Just a Little Bit

ANN TOMPERT Illustrated by Lynn Munsinger

HOUGHTON MIFFLIN COMPANY

BOSTON

ATLANTA   DALLAS   GENEVA, ILLINOIS   PALO ALTO   PRINCETON

For Julie — A.T.
For Wulf — L.M.

Just a Little Bit, by Ann Tompert, illustrated by Lynn Munsinger. Text copyright © 1993 by Ann Tompert. Illustrations copyright © 1993 by Lynn Munsinger. Reprinted by permission of Houghton Mifflin Company. All rights reserved.

Houghton Mifflin Edition, 1997

Printed in the U.S.A.

ISBN: 0-395-81083-3

123456789-B-02 01 00 99 98 97 96

Elephant and Mouse were in the park, playing on the
slides and swings. Elephant said, "Let's try the seesaw."

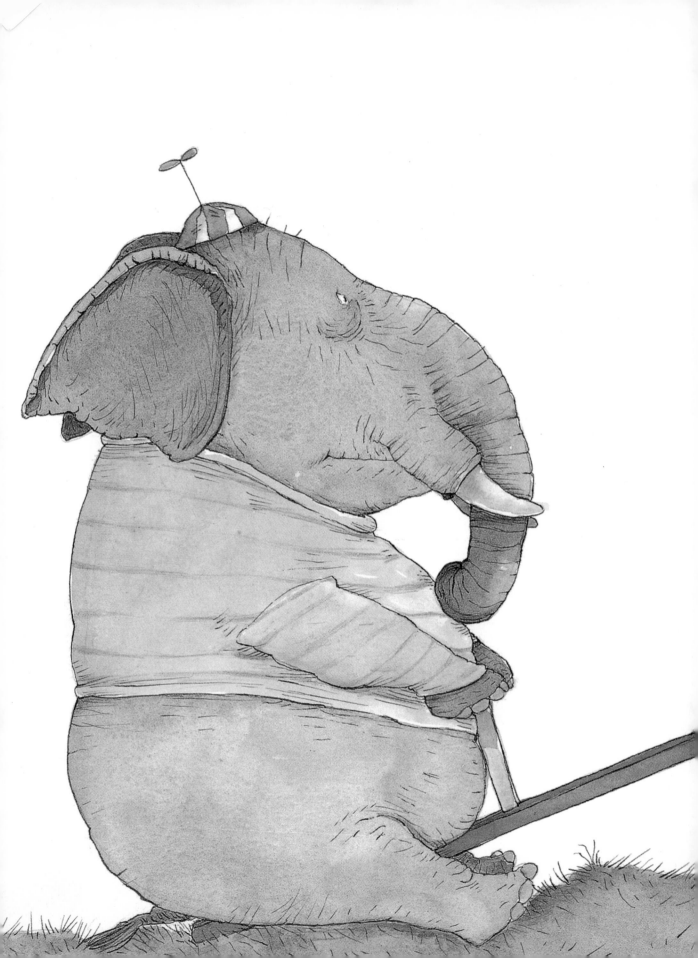

Elephant sat on the down side of the seesaw. Mouse climbed to the very edge of the up side. But nothing happened.

"Push down," urged Elephant. "Push down."

Mouse pushed down against the board as hard as he could. Still, nothing happened.

Along came Giraffe.
"Let me help you," she said.

Giraffe walked up the board and sat next to Mouse. Nothing happened. Elephant's end of the seesaw stayed on the ground. Mouse's end stayed in the air.

"You need just a little bit more help," said Zebra,
trotting up the seesaw.
And—nothing happened.

Elephant still stayed on the ground. Mouse still stayed in the air.

"You need just a little bit more help,"
said Lion, and he pranced up the seesaw.
And—nothing happened.

"Everyone together now," urged Elephant.
"Push down!"

Mouse, Giraffe, Zebra, and Lion pushed down with all their might.

And — nothing happened.

By then a crowd had gathered to watch.

"I need just a little bit more help," Elephant called out to them.

"Let me see what I can do," said Bear.
As he lumbered up the seesaw toward them,
Mouse, Giraffe, Zebra, and Lion grunted
and groaned and grimaced as they pressed
down on the board with every last
bit of their strength.

And—nothing happened.

"Oh, no," moaned the crowd.

"Who will help me just a little bit more?" Elephant called out to the crowd.

"How about me?" cried Crocodile.

"And me?" said Mongoose.

"I'll join the party," called Monkey from the banana tree overhead. She swung down onto Ostrich's back.

Crocodile, Mongoose, Monkey, and Ostrich climbed
onto the seesaw, one at a time.
And—nothing happened.
"Oh, no," moaned the crowd again.

"He'll never get off the ground," said someone
in the crowd.

"Push down! Push down!" urged Elephant.

Mouse, Giraffe, Zebra, Lion, Bear, Crocodile,
Mongoose, Monkey, and Ostrich grunted
and groaned and grimaced as they all pushed
down on the board as hard as they could.
And—nothing happened.

"They'll never do it," said someone in the crowd.
"Let's go!"
The onlookers had started to move away when a small brown beetle flew down from the sky. For a moment it hovered above the seesaw. Then it flew straight to Mouse and landed on his head.

Down, down, down to the ground went
Mouse and the rest of the animals.
"Every little bit helps!" Elephant trumpeted
from the top of the seesaw.

"Hurray! Hurray! Hurray!" cheered the crowd.

With Elephant on one side and Mouse, Giraffe, Zebra, Lion, Bear, Crocodile, Mongoose, Monkey, Ostrich, and the small brown beetle on the other, they all went up and down, up and down, while the crowd cheered and clapped.